Table of Contents

the sound of pigs falling	7
nation	8
index	10
learning to learn	18
death speaks ordinary language	19
'is there anywhere a force ... ?'	20
rough work	21
the shopping mall is burning	23
found event	25
Stefan George	26
Soviet Factory	27
money	28
the unground enters	29
the sun reddens	30
I am instructed	31
animalia	32
illuminist	33
thanks Jeff	34
homage to Trilce XIII	35
loathsome familiarity	36
bundled	37
outlived lives	38

spot the early signs of madness   39

the king's speech   40

you are the gatekeeper   41

Bill knocked out   42

condition of hope   43

beyond desire another day   44

'Bring back that black thing ...   45

frontal lobe   46

clock is natal sack   47

slow acid   48

pale light flares   49

Royal Palace   50

always mesmerized by the parst   51

a gel of time   52

now / awaken   53

you yourself a stranger   54

hard as stone   55

plasm-sac   56

for Sean   57

'property makes us stupid'   58

subject to light   59

how out of life   60

more sacrificed women   61

on   63

growth   65

To NGC and FGR

the sound of pigs falling

the sound of pigs falling
has fallen out of words
///dear dead///
some next-level revolution coming
cancels your silence
punching holes in the name of things
which body
from our bodies fall
the people armed
never be
mystical dreams
in other words
exceeds
its representation
poetry is a virus
mutating
right in
front
of your face

nation

'they find nostalgia, they find heritage, in the nation state.'

– Sir Simon Jenkins

thought stop money thought some
money thought money

some money thought money

thought money thought

the gass
passes through

fiery green
day breaks
what utopia

the stars grim on their black stalks
all of them polar opposites is
corporate synthesis

impunity
layer upon layer

is our alphabet
dead radio voices
in the sun

I am seeing something else
irrefutable insect survival
secret endless food

it's empty mate

the body is
being dead
had fallen out of words

lack of courage is
stopping me from writing

I am flayed
with water and sparrows

I walk away from a university
with a delayed dictionary

sterile zone
peripheral buffer

it's the year
of the Olympics

index

there's someone
whose need is reversed

the air is full
of the cries of men and women
signals
expunged unexpunged

the air is his book

chained to the morning
already cast early sky ribs
the same thing rising

nothing is missing

Carpetright

Post Office

Boots

JD Sports

O2

Currys

Argos

PC World

Comet

H&M

HMV

Haringey Magistrate's Court

Haringey Shopping Centre

Gay's the Word

Aldi

H&M

JD Sports

Fire engine

Fire engine

Carphone Warehouse

T-Mobile

Design Studio

Fire engine

JD Sports

Argos

MacDonalds

W H Smith

Blockbuster

Tesco

Tottenham Hotspur Football Club

Kelmscott Secondary School

Dalston Kingsland Centre

Bus and police cars

Foot Locker

Halfords

Currys

Police Car

Sainsbury's

Police car

Valens Jewellers

Ozcam Jewellers

JD Sports

Sainsbury's

Savers

Foot Locker

Carphone Warehouse

Evans Cycles

Jamie's Italian

Currys

Halfords

Brazas Restaurant National Express bus

Sony Distribution Centre

Palisades Shopping Centre

Bullring Shopping Centre

Pure Gym

Tesco

Addidas

Ealing Broadway Station

Tottenham Centre Retail Park

Jessops

Game

Police car

JD Sports

Argos

Harveys

Mothercare

JD Sports

Debenhams

Burger King

Ladbrokes

Bus

Argos

Betfred

Sainsbury's

Topshop

Argos

O2

Carphone Warehouse

Phone 4U

Cash Converters

Foot Locker

Boots

Barclays

The Ledbury

MacDonalds

Reading Angling Centre

Greggs

Cyber Candy

Richer Sounds

Money Shop

Diesel

Bang & Olafsen

Swarovski

Tesco Express

Bromley South Station

Argos

Primark

Arndale Centre

Foot Asylum

Bargain Booze

Miss Selfridge

Square Peg Pub

Orange

Reeves

T-Mobile

Austin Reed

Jessops

MacDonald's

Thomas Sabo

Admiral Street Police Station

Tesco Express

Jamaica Inn

Cabot Circus Shopping Centre

Gas main

Vodafone

Clarence Convenience Store

Clarks

Primark

H Pollock

Salford Shopping City

3 Mobile

Ugg

Meadows Police Station

Job Centre

Macro

Great Harry Pub

Coral

Sainsburys

Life

Canning Circus Police Station

Marks & Spencer

Orange

Patisserie Valerie

Kro Bar

Café Nero

Burton

Pretty Green

Picadilly Museums

Wimpy

Charles Dance Jewellers

No1 Pizza

House of Fraser

JD Sports

Liver Launderette

Belal's Newsagent

ASDA

ASDA

Bloc Inc

Jessops

something strictly unnameable
happens to the image of suffering
and what this has to do with riot
by previously existing criminals
political and final stone

learning to learn

learning
to hear
the dispute within the waves

Whitman too

could hear the stems
thrusting through the earth

but the line of fire in the street
still burning burns

utopian fire

feel the joy of appetite
in blood and fire

interrupt
the boundless azure

gaze of the rulers
all the pores of hatred open

pour a line of petrol on the street
it'll keep the police busy

death speaks ordinary language

death speaks ordinary language
civilisation stuff
what will be the fulcrum of my eyes?

how discover
political action
with the humans on our backs

I am accompanied by someone else
it needs to be
how to kill
written on the air

'is there anywhere a force strong enough to put an end to this state of affairs?'

– Hugo Ball

the walls of the cell

time hardens

demands a vast theatre

the person breaks out of life

fierce moments

innumerable rays

the situation

not coded or decoded / or

opaque or transparent

the money signifier / is one of

semblance

then find a better one

I am heading towards certain

territories

hooliganed

it's december always

at the repair place

rough work

to grasp an opportunity in the
current abyss instead of
submitting to the wreck of our
common life by clinging to the
old meanings / what's to be
done with

an apparition which has a left
hand

a glue so simple it sticks
memory to good intention with
ideas of repair

it's the false beloved

a warm and mild apparition

like so many obsolete
compounds

like opinion

there is an absolute moment of
composition which grasps the
void of this situation

revolution

revolution anyway

the shopping mall is burning

the shopping mall is burning
end of my silence
my slot perspectives
scopic error
cream suck
non-conjunction and non-disjunction
infants used as signs
here are real repairs
sends the runner
something good appear
imagine reference from words
when to shift gaze
integrated discrete programme
time-shifted vocabulary of learning

there is nothing to do
there is only the effort to wake up
and the possibility you won't
it has already happened several times
before the person can think or know
who shehe is
the cloned

eyes go to sleep

is voices   and is not

new forms of barbarism

or general emancipation

found event

by entering the event
you give your express consent
for your actual or simulated likeness
to be included in any and all media
for any purpose at any time
this includes filming by the police

Stefan George

shadows of the sea
   stiff surf
       still sky
   the pretence of the day

   the bride wrapped in silence

       chords of spray

   voices calling

   the dazzling crown of words

and
the militarization of space
has already happened

Soviet Factory

the Red Flag Textile Factory St Petersburg
photographed by Richard Pare 1999
an image
of hope
(gone ((gone) (((lost
and did it smell like this then?

money

money

        walking around

smell / washed out

orgasm and
other colours

the unground enters

a complex of hole agencies and obscure
surfaces unground the earth . . . once
freed from its solar slavery the
earth can rise against the Sun
and its solar capitalism

that we should be so lucky

the sun reddens

the sun reddens
it interdicts itself
the silence reddens

I am instructed

I am instructed in space and affect

to curse the event

the intense common light

dawn in dawn light

bad eye movement

incarceration

animalia

the language of the dice

the hot disease I hear

turns

to exile

an appropriate obsessing technique

like natural

to the natural orifice

office

into her body they put you again

explicit monsters

they put you into your body again

syntax

gang

convulsive writing

dilates the

genitals

on the other slope

dice speak

illuminist

so many instruments
 dreamed
of a thing not
 dreamed
mud-coloured flesh
 I'm so glad so glad
it's the sound of human sound
 water breaking
all the beings that exist in the water will die
 hence the need for their illumination
produces rapid eye movement
 produces movement
cars burning in Paris suburbs
 conflagrations
exact calibrations of injustice
 it's the 20th of October
the frenzy of youth

thanks Jeff

what I was the   organ

what I want was

I want to be that thing

there is no explanation

homage to Trilce XIII

a mere furrow
it is and remains
immortal
I worship Kunt
all my death

loathsome familiarity

loathsome familiarity
of the sex partner
the interminable abyss
can't be said or removed either
the false evening
what it said

bundled

bundled
by wild yellow or gold
faster than word sounds
my reason for
turning away from them

outlived lives

what does it mean
to do the thing
which exceeds everything
for eternal purposes
drive through the actual gas
the outgoing screams
vacating something that's
even the frame
((even the furnace

spot the early signs of madness

spot the early signs of madness
keep the person a little bit longer
I'm not worried if you're not worried

if you're worried see your doctor
for symptoms caused by damage and loss

remember past events and problems
hard to follow tv programmes

spot the early
signal of your
dementia

the king's speech

he did learn to speak
but could not say
a single true word
even with the help
of Winston Churchill
and Simon Schama
and Rowan Williams
etc.

you are the gatekeeper

you are the gatekeeper
you are the interior trace of hunger
gaslight in a glass column
the inheritor, the tree
enjoyment of this society
as someone who has always died
will eternally be ripped off
by the corrupting demons of the air

Bill knocked out

his disgust

for disgust

his pain unbound

departure for new affection and wound

the line refraction

of something that

if hell

speaks

prevents that thing from being seen

but the soft drill

of the poem

ah reader

the small swirl of letters

touches it

they

were of the party of death

dust and rain in the gutter

who can stop its arrow

condition of hope

the air in sunlight and beyond
the line that is waiting
a swerve away from them
during the colour of the sky
will always shine like clouds
a kiss away
from palaces of the real
always outside itself
we are 2 in evening
the complex lens
the evening at last
pale mauve or whisky
the strata of the air
after rain
indistinct
distinct

beyond desire another day

rich unattached rib
rises even in night
my previous contents
in the time place
exit into morning

'Bring back that black thing
we did not have in our story'

the dusk leaves and shadows leave
light without shadow
no name
hallucinates them
1,700 drones
the wrong man
our thousand year plan
despair
air

frontal lobe

frontal lobe
is powerful new real and

lesion offer
cannot help us grasp it

being and shit

take part
share every human emotion

the actual screen
being luminous in the afternoon

the glow of capital

can you see it?

clock is natal sack

clock is natal sac
how you do do it
ruts in and in the river
always mirror mirror
yellow money
(how systems kill you
never worry)
always equilibrium
in the supreme presence
supreme police

the animal in the sawdust
kills time

slow acid

slow acid
ha!

it's the emotion
late dawn suicide

varios objetos
gone and gone
happiness again
casi forever

far away
from any actual thing

like being blue in the sky
like sex

everywhere

pale light flares

pale light flares
from the phenomenological plants
unfailing light
realistic music

too high a price

Royal Palace

royal apartments
royal medals
royals doing sport
royal toys
royal babies
princes doing sprache

abajo
la turbulencia incalculable de la lengua

always mesmerized by the parst

if i stayed in everlarsting time
i'd still have a little fuck

if we exit under money
the shit language hoovers life

our own
political thing

a gel of time

a gel of time
outer edge: saline

that man was in
the idea of myself
inside my bones

you have to be fearless
to put the beats
where he put them

turning up his red lamp
the years are stolen
there can be no negation
so that an old man may be born
silence become silence
the words closer

the real edge of fear is
'the real sound of the dead'
or are the wishes of the dead
for positive recognition
white and armless signals
seagulls?

now / awaken

now

awaken

into the head of the colonisers

put that in your frontal lobe

hellboy in your name to be

your frontal bone

make a curvature of

time against the

regime of

progress is oven

a social revolt

against the wind of time is blowing

murders

what your needs

actually are

brothers and sisters

you yourself a stranger

you yourself a stranger in that night
in the low glow of tv
resurrect the dead from winter
their mouths popping louder than names
faithful to you and not to any other
confidence in the ladder and not in the steps
in you and not in any other

hard as stone

for many days summer even in winter
the weird spine
the glow of that book
seen with this specter in its mouth
red segment
air of other wounds
ruining the mouth
without possible animal
what you do understand
so entirely without hope
ah gypsies
bitter yellow
don't trust the redeemers
where you do live the dead
continually and hissingly
the time fragment
related or unattended
music hard as stone

plasm-sac

the white material
enters the lunacy period
the pigeons walk along the edges reading
the bought environment
the edges disappear

for Sean

'There is a moment in each day that Satan cannot find'

– Blake, *Milton*

strong psychic instru-

ment marks

chaos marks

political si-

lence penetra-

tes ruins of sound

where it dis-

appears

out of mind

that could

hold hell

this is

shattered city

'property makes us stupid'

what obscure
Courage what
Illumination how
blind could
see in
Property the
formless
and
reduced Beings
a memory
Gin repeatable
Theatre of
Wound less
than Violence
and more

subject to light

subject to light

the opium abstract

cancellation of luminous detail

song of the helicopter dawn

the slow segments of fury

promethean speed

materials necessary to produce the time

fallen out of systems

parts of themselves

suicidal time

the roar of that dimension

how out of life

how out of life
series too
is ripped out of series
tears from ---------------- disappeared
to ------------------------ disappeared

the wound says nothing
held the rudder
of that conception

the idea of
silence moving any faster

organised
in the
non-word

thought wants
to survive

you can only read the score
if   you   are death

more sacrificed women

A la sombra de los estucos
llegan viejos y zancos
en sus mamelucos
los vampiros blancos.

in the shadow of plastered
walls here come
in their suits
the long-legged white vampires.

– José María Eguren, 'La diosa ambarina'.

what is mysterious

if the rain mocks and mocks

mocks and bellows

could the thing heard

not have known

if the word was

bootless volume

so the ones who die

without being born

snuffed

ah west wind

I am eight years old
every word hates hurts

more sacrificed women

on

sit in the
hospital it is
sitting for
something a
strong smell
already the
smell has
gone through
everything
this is the
stiff cuffs of
the nurses
and her cold
white hand
also the
brown walls
stiff white
virgins and
instruments
of your
present time
courage and
he lack of it

has passed
through all
the bodies
including the
father inside
the mother
and how it
might not be
this how we
might spit it
out lying on
a rubber
sheet and
how it might
grow into
you the thing
you choke
on

growth

the three black fans at the back of
some London buses, which you can
see from the top deck of another
bus, have a sinister look, they seem
to be looking back at you.
functionally, if you think about it,
rationally, they must have to do
with ventilation in hot weather. but
what is the function of the function?
in november, they weren't turning,
though you could see the blades
were black. in appearance they
indicate the fans of some larger
ducts, like the ones that prevent a
factory combusting and killing the
workers. what is the larger
machine? for example, the fans that
ventilate some of the tube tunnels
are much larger, perhaps two or
three metres tall. to blow enough air
so that passengers can breathe. or
the fans you can see through the
intake of a jet engine: at least two

metres high, and think of the
quantity of air that is compressed
and pushed through them. and the
wind that ventilates the city, is it
enough? the huge invisible fans. the
ducts.